Listen to the Land

(Historical Gography)

Dr. Cyndi Parker

BiblicalTraining.org
Because Your Spiritual Growth Matters

Overview

Title: Listen to the Land

Speaker: Dr. Cyndi Parker

I. GOALS

1. Learn how the rocks, roads and geographical features affected the lives of the people of the Bible.

2. Gain insight into the imagery and metaphors that the biblical writers used as they recorded and prophesied events.

3. Understand the connection of significant locations and landmarks in the Old Testament and New Testament.

IV. REQUIREMENTS

1. 21 sessions
2. 16 hours total

III. PREREQUISITES

None

IV. FORMAT

Video/Audio

BiblicalTraining.org

BiblicalTraining.org is not-for-profit ministry that gives all people access to a world-class Christian education at no cost. Our classes range from new believers to biblical literacy ("Foundations"), deeper Bible study ("Academy"), and seminary-level training ("Institute").

We are a 501(c)3 not-for-profit and rely solely on the donations of our users. All donations are tax deductible according to the current US tax codes.

I. DISTINCTIVES

World class. All Bible classes are taught by world-class professors from major seminaries.

Holistic. We want to see students move through content to deep reflection and application.

Configurable. Ministries can use BT lectures as well as their own to design their educational program.

Accessible. BiblicalTraining is a web-based ministry whose content is provided at no cost.

Community-based. We encourage people to learn together, in mentor/apprentice relationships.

Broadly evangelical. Our materials are broadly evangelical, governed by our Statement of Faith, and are not tied to any one church, denomination or tradition.

Partners. We provide the content and delivery mechanisms, and our partner organizations provide the community and mentoring.

Table of Contents

Overview iii

BiblicalTraining.org iv

Table of Contents. v

Your Speaker vii

Weekly schedule viii

Mentor's Guide ix

1. Introduction 1

2. Rivers and Roads 5

3. Climate, Resources and Calendar 14

4. Rocks and Soil 24

5. The Transjordan 31

6. Coastal Plain and Negev 38

7. The Rift Valley and Jericho 48

8. Hill Country of Judah 57

9. Historical Background of Jerusalem 62

10. Jerusalem in the First Century 68

11. Benjamin 73

12. The Shephelah 76

13. The Sharon Plain and Mount Carmel 82

14. The Hill Country of Joseph 88

15. Samaria 93

16. Acco Plain 98

17. Jezreel and Herod Valleys 103

18. Sea of Galilee 110

19. Huleh Basin 119

20. Going Out From the Land 125

21. Epilogue 129

Your Speaker

Dr. Cyndi Parker holds a Ph.D. in Theological and Religious Studies from the University of Gloucestershire and teaches in churches and universities around the world. Dr. Parker lived in Jerusalem for five years and currently teaches courses about the geographical, cultural, religious, and political context of the Bible at Jerusalem University College.

She has led over forty trips in Israel, and she continues to develop innovative educational trips to Israel, seeking to inspire students of all ages through experiential education. Her research interests include biblical views of Place, Biblical History and Geography, and the correlation between Theology and Ecology (with a particular interest in Food Justice). She is the owner of www.NarrativeofPlace.com, the author of *Encountering Jesus in the Real World of the Gospels*, and the host of the *Context Matters* podcast.

I. EDUCATION

Ph.D., University of Gloucestershire

M.A.

B.A.

We are pleased that you have chosen to use materials from BiblicalTraining.org. We trust that you will find them to be of the highest quality and truly helpful in your own spiritual growth and that of your church. Please read through the following guidelines; they will help you make the best use of this guide.

Weekly schedule

Listen or watch the lesson. The lesson for each chapter is designed to be listened to outside of your meeting. Each lesson lasts for an hour. This is a crucial step. If the meeting time with your fellow students is going to be productive and encouraging, everyone in the group needs to have listened to and wrestled with the lesson.

Take notes. This guide has the outline for each lesson with a summary of the teaching for each major point. If you are unable to take notes while listening to the lesson, please work through the guide at some point before your meeting.

Questions. Each chapter closes with a series of questions. Some of the questions are data based, confirming that you understand the information. Other questions are more reflective, helping you move beyond the important accumulation of knowledge to challenging you to think through what you are learning about God, yourself and others, and finally to application. Our encouragement is to think through your answers before your meeting and then use the meeting to share your thoughts and interact with others.

Meeting. Meet together with your group.

II.   MEETING TOGETHER

While some people may have to study on their own, we strongly recommend finding a group with which you can study.

A group provides encouragement to finish the class.

Interacting with others, their understanding and insight, is the most effective way to sharpen your own thoughts and beliefs.

Just as you will need the help of others from time to time, so also they will need your help.

Mentor's Guide

If you are leading the group or mentoring an individual, here are some suggestions that should help you.

Your role is to facilitate. This is not an opportunity for you to teach. In fact, the less visible role you take, the better. Your role is to listen and bring out the best in the other people.

Preparation. Be sure to have done your homework thoroughly. Have listened to the lesson and think carefully through the questions. Have an answer for each question that will get the conversation going. A great question is, "What is the Lord teaching you this week?"

Creativity. What works to help one person understand may not help another. So listen to the conversation and pray that the Lord help you bring out the greatest interaction among all the people.

Correct error. This is difficult. If someone says something that isn't right, you don't want to come down on them, telling them they are wrong and shutting down their participation. On the other hand, if you let an obvious error pass, the rest of the group may think you agree and what was said was correct. So look for gracious ways to suggest that perhaps the person's comment was incorrect.

Focus. Stay focused on Jesus and the Bible, not on church or religious traditions.

Lead the discussion. People don't want to listen to a sharing of common ignorance. Lead by asking questions that will prompt others to think.

Silence. Don't be afraid of silence. It may mean nothing more than people are thinking. But if the conversation lags, then ask thought-provoking questions to get the discussion started, and then step out of the way.

Discipleship. Be acutely aware of how you can mentor the people in the group. Meet with them for coffee. Share some life with them. Jesus' Great Commission is to teach people to obey, and the only way this happens is in relationship.

Different perspectives. People process information and express themselves in different ways based on their background, previous experience, culture, religion and other factors. Encourage an atmosphere that allows people to share honestly and respectfully.

Privacy. All discussions are private, not to be shared outside the group unless otherwise specified.

Goal. The goal of this study is not just increased knowledge; it is transformation. Don't be content with people getting the "right" answers. The Pharisees got the "right" answer, and many of them never made it to heaven (Matt 5:20).

Relationships. Share everyone's name, email and phone number so people can communicate during the week and follow up on prayer requests. You may want to set up a way to share throughout the week using Slack or WhatsApp.

Finish well. Encourage the people to make the necessary commitment to do the work, think reflectively over the questions, and complete the class.

Prayer. Begin and end every meeting with prayer. Please don't do the quick "one-prayer-covers-all" approach. Manage the time so all of you can pray over what you have learned and with what you have been challenged. Pray regularly for each individual in the meeting.

1

Introduction

I. LANDSCAPE PICTURES

II. BIBLICAL WRITERS USED THEIR LANDSCAPE

The places in which the Bible narratives took place affected the stories

III. PSALM 23

Your interpretation of the Bible is affected by the assumptions you make

A. Topography

Physical geographical details

B. Toponymy

Link between the historical record and the landscape

C. Archaeology

Studying history through excavation of sites and analysis of artifacts

REFLECTION QUESTIONS

1. Think of a couple of places that have different geography and climate, for instance a Scandinavian country and an equatorial island nation. Think of the different lifestyles, food, cultures, customs and worldviews they would have. Which places in Israel have different climates and geography? How will that affect their lifestyle, occupation, politics, relationships, etc.?

2. The biblical writers used their landscape to explain their theology. When you read the Bible, you fill in those pictures and analogies with what you are familiar with. What is the danger in that? How can understanding the geography help with this problem?

3. When you think about God being your shepherd in Psalm 23, how does imagining sheep in a lush fenced pasture rather than out in the open in an arid wilderness area change your theology and your relationship with God?

4. What does "geography cannot prove the Bible, but the events of the Bible are not disproved by it" mean? Do you think the Bible is trustworthy? Why or why not?

5. What is archaeology? What is the process archaeologists use to get artifacts that they can examine? How does this help to get more information about events that are recorded in the Bible?

2

Rivers and Roads

I. PROMINENT RIVERS IN THE ANCIENT NEAR EAST

A. Tigris and Euphrates Rivers

Assyria, Babylon, Persia

B. Nile River

Egypt

II. BENEFITS OF RIVERS

A. Agriculture flourishes

Abundant water, good soil and favorable climate

B. Facilitates trade

Transporting commodities and people

C. Resources for nation building

Surplus commodities and trade

D. Major empires in the Ancient Near East

Egypt, Assyria, Babylon, Persia

III. ISRAEL

A. Textured

Hills, valleys, mountains and rivers

B. No major river

The Jordan river is comparatively small

C. Trade routes

Connection between Fertile Crescent and Egypt

IV. GOD'S CALL OF ABRAHAM

A. Culture

Abraham leaves family, gods and land

B. Geography

Israel can have an influence on everyone passing through

V. GEOGRAPHICAL BIG PICTURE

A. Longitudinal zones

1. Coastal Plain

Land bordering the Mediterranean coast

2. Central Mountain

Upper Galilee to Biblical Negev

3. Rift Valley

Huleh Basin to the Red Sea

4. Transjordan

East of the Jordan River

B. East-West connections

1. Jezreel and Harod Valley

North, near Mt. Carmel

2. Biblical Negev

Some flat areas and narrow valleys

C. Roads

1. International roads

Travel between fertile crescent and Egypt

2. Israelite roads

Local travel and commerce

3. Neighbors

Conflict over control of international roads

4. Solomon

City location is strategic

REFLECTION QUESTIONS

1. What is the value of using your own map when you are studying the Bible?

2. What were the nations that existed near the Nile, Tigris and Euphrates Rivers? What enabled them to become dominant political and military empires?

3. Since Israel did not have the resources to become dominant militarily or economically, in what way does the geography give Israel the opportunity to have an impact on the whole known world? How is Ezekiel 27 an example of this? How does Jesus model this in his ministry? How is this a model for the way that you can have an impact in your sphere of relationships?

4. What are the three things that God asks Abram to leave in Genesis 12:1-2? Why are these particularly significant in the culture in which Abram lived? As God called Abram to have faith to follow him, in what ways is God calling you to live by faith in your life?

5. What road does Joseph use to travel to find his brothers? What town are they in when he meets up with them? Why is that significant for Joseph ending up in Egypt?

6. What are the cities that Solomon built that are listed in 1 Kings 9:15? What is significant about their location? How does this contribute to Solomon's accumulation of power and wealth?

3

Climate, Resources and Calendar

I. RESOURCES

A. Wind and rain

Wind brings the moisture in from the Mediterranean

A. Rules of rainfall

More rainfall on the west side of the hills than on the east side

II. CALENDAR

A. Two seasons

Rainy and dry seasons

B. Thirst of the land

Water management techniques

C. Cycle of the crops

Grains harvested early in the year

D. Sheep

Sheep eat the stubble after the grain harvest

E. Late summer dew

Dew settles in the morning then evaporates when the sun comes out

F. Fruit harvest

Late in the year

III. BIBLICAL PASSAGES

A. Deuteronomy 8:7-10

A good land

B. Luke 2:8

Time of year of the birth of Jesus

IV. THREE FESTIVALS

A. Passover

Beginning of the barley harvest

B. Shavuot

After the grain harvests

C. Succoth

Feast of booths

D. John 7:37-38

Jesus offers water at the time of the year when people are thirsty

REFLECTION QUESTIONS

1. What areas in Israel get more rainfall? Why? What limits the areas that are good for agriculture besides rainfall? What strategies do people use to overcome these limitations?

2. What do people raise in areas that don't have enough rainfall for agricultural crops? Why does this work?

3. What are the rules of rainfall? What areas have more rainfall and which have less? What causes this? What difference does this make in the way people live in these areas?

4. Why is the calendar drawn in a circular shape? What does this tell you about how the ancient people viewed the passing of time? How is that different from modern cultures?

5. How many seasons are in the ancient calendar? What are they? What characterizes the weather during these seasons? What happens during the transitions between the seasons? Why is this important?

6. What is the meaning of Jeremiah 5:24? How does understanding the ancient calendar help you to understand the meaning of the passage?

6. How is a spring formed? Why is it referred to as "living water?" Why is this a metaphor that Jesus chose to describe himself? In what ways is this true of your relationship with God?

7. How did people create a well? In what ways was it significant to a community?

8. How did people make cisterns? How are they designed? What are the risks involved in the way the water is collected and in the way that the use of the water is managed? How is that a different mindset from people who have an abundance of running water available to them? How does this help you understand the power of the imagery that Jeremiah uses in Jeremiah 2:13?

9. In what ways did it benefit both the people who raised crops and the people who raised animals to work together?

10. What is the agricultural benefit of the dew that comes in late summer? How is this used as imagery in a positive way in Deuteronomy chapter 32? How is it used in a negative way by some of the prophets? Can you think of a specific verse that is meaningful to you that uses "dew" as a metaphor?

11. In Deuteronomy 8:7-10, how does Moses use references to the agricultural calendar to indicate how God will bless the people of Israel? In what ways has God blessed you? In what ways has it motivated you to seek him and serve him?

12. How does an understanding of the agricultural calendar help you to use the details in Luke 2:8 to determine in what time of year Jesus was likely born?

13. What is happening in the agricultural calendar during the feast of Passover? How is this related to the first Passover?

14. What is happening in the agricultural calendar during the feast of Shavuot? What event is this feast related to in the history of the people of Israel?

15. What is happening in the agricultural calendar during the feast of Succoth? What part of the history of the people of Israel is this related to? What did they do to celebrate it?

16. How does understanding the agricultural calendar and the way that the people of Israel celebrate Succoth give you a more complete understanding of John 8:37-38? How have you experienced in your life, this promise that Jesus made?

4

Rocks and Soil

I. LAYERS OF ROCK

A. Cenomanian

Mineral content is good for agriculture

B. Senonian

Chalky soil that supports herders

C. Eocene

Chalk and Nari crust

D. Volcanic soil

Found in the north

II.   THE "GOOD" LAND OF MILK AND HONEY

A. Milk

Sheep's milk

A. Honey

Possibly date palms

B. Deuteronomy 11:9-15

How to live with God in the place you have been
given

III. WHAT DO WE CALL THIS LAND?

A. Dan to Beersheba

Dan in the north and Beersheba in the south

B. Holy Land

The land where the narrative of God interacting with
his people unfolded

C. Palestine

A term used beginning with the Romans

D. Israel

Political boundaries are fluid

E. Levant

Europe-centric

F. Land Between

Descriptive of the way the land functions

REFLECTION QUESTIONS

1. What are the three kinds of rocks that primarily make up the layers of sediment that have been laid down over time?

2. What are the three layers of limestone in order from top to bottom? What causes these layers to be different thicknesses and exposed in different ways in different places?

3. What are the characteristics of Cenomanian limestone? What uses do these characteristics promote? What kinds of rock formations are often created? What is the name of the soil that is created when this rock breaks down?

4. What are the characteristics of Senonian limestone? What is the name of the soil that is created when it breaks down? What lifestyle activities does this soil support?

5. What are the characteristics of Eocene? What soil is created when it erodes?

6. What type of rock is created by volcanic activity? What are the characteristics of this type of rock? In what area of the country is it often found?

7. What does the phrase, "land of milk and honey" mean? What might milk and honey refer to individually?

8. How does Deuteronomy 11:9-15 describe living in the land as being different from living in Egypt? How will the "sense of agency" be different? How will this affect the way the people of Israel live their lives? What does this teach you about how God wants you to live your life? What is a way you can put that into practice today?

9. What are different names that people use to refer to this land? What does Dr. Parker prefer? Why?

5

The Transjordan

I. BASHAN

Northwest region

II. GILEAD

A. Geography

Dome of Gilead connection points

B. Ammonites

Neighbors of Israel

III. MISHOR AND MOAB

A. Moab

South of the Arnon River

B. Two international roads

Two routes on either side of the plain

C. Origin of the people of Moab

Descendants of one of Lot's daughters

IV. EDOM

A. Soil and geography

Sandstone and wilderness

B. Origin of the people of Edom

Descendants of Esau

REFLECTION QUESTIONS

1. What is the name of the area near the Yarmuk River? Why is the line of sight unrestricted in major parts of this area? How does this affect the attitudes of the people living there?

2. What type of soil is common in this area? What are some areas difficult to farm? What is commonly raised here?

3. What references do other biblical writers make when referring to Bashan?

4. What points of connection are there in Gilead? What geographical features make this possible? What non-Israel people group is in this area?

5. What type of rock is exposed on the Dome of Gilead? What nearby area has soil and climate that is similar to this?

6. What is the origin of the Ammonites? In Deuteronomy 2:19, how does God instruct the people of Israel to treat the Ammonites? Why?

7. Where is the Mishor region in relation to the Dome of Gilead? What type of landscape is it? What is the predominant type of soil? What is this region good for raising?

8. What is the difference in terrain of the two international roads going through Moab? What would cause you to choose one over the other?

9. What types of soil are visible in Edom? What color is it?

10. What is the meaning of the word, "Seir?" What are possible reasons why this is descriptive of this area and the origins of the people who live there?

11. What is the primary economic activity in Edom? Why?

12. What is the origin of the people of Edom? How is this related to God's promise to Hagar in Genesis 16? What does God tell the people of Israel about how they should treat the people of Edom as they are approaching the promised land?

6

Coastal Plain and Negev

V. COASTAL PLAIN

A. Roads

Two sections of the international road

B. Soil

Alluvial

VI. ORIGIN OF THE PHILISTINES

A. The "sea" people

From Macedonia

B. The pentapolis

Five capital cities

C. Early conflict with the people of Israel

Battle at Ebenezer

VII. NEGEV

A. Kadesh Barnea

The place where the 12 spies go into the land

B. Texture

The "knuckles" of the Negev

VIII. BIBLICAL NEGEV

A. Soil and climate

Loess soil, minimal rainfall

B. Wadi Besor

Large system with fingers from the hills

C. Roads

Flat and wide roads

D. Beer-sheba

Abraham dug a well and planted a tree

E. Arad

Founded before Abraham

F. Queen of Sheba

Possibly motivated by future trade

G. Edom

Edom always wanted to control the Negev for trade

REFLECTION QUESTIONS

1. Describe the location of the two segments of the international road in the Philistine coastal plain. Why do they rejoin into one road in the northern part of this area?

2. What type of soil is in this area? What processes produced this soil? What were crops that were commonly raised here?

3. What caused the coastal part of the international road to be inland from the shore? Why was their shipping activity limited?

4. Where did the Philistines come from? How many capital cities did they have? Where were the cities strategically located?

5. What does the word Negev mean? What is the average rainfall? What can be raised here?

6. What is at Kadesh Barnea that would cause people to stop there? Why was this a significant place for the people of Israel before they went into the promised land?

7. How does Dr. Parker describe the texture of the greater Negev? What causes most of the erosion? In what way is this descriptive of how Job refers to the way his "friends" are treating him?

8. Where is the Biblical Negev located? Why is it a place that people in Biblical times wanted to control and have access to it?

9. What kind of soil will you find there? What can be raised here?

10. What cities are near the Wadi Besor? Where does the water it collects drain into? What does Genesis 26:16-23 tell you about the lifestyle and the water resources of the people here?

11. Which road passes through the biblical Negev? How does that explain the nationalities of people that live here?

12. What kind of tree does Abraham plant near Beer-sheba? Why is it significant? How is this city related to the story of Hagar?

13. In what ways was Beer-sheba an important city in the nation of Israel? What did archaeologists find there that is related to this?

14. How did ancient people build the city of Arad to make it habitable? How did the nation of Israel use it?

15. Where did the Queen of Sheba live in relation to Israel? What was her likely economic reason for visiting Solomon?

16. Why did Edom want access and control over the biblical Negev? How did they accomplish it?

7

The Rift Valley and Jericho

I. RIFT VALLEY

A. Aravah

Springs and copper mines

B. Dead Sea

Minerals but no agriculture

C. Bitumen

Used to caulk ships and for medicines

D. Balsam

The sap was valuable enough to export

E. Masada

Island of rock

F. En Gedi

Collection of springs

II. JERICHO

A. Herod and Cleopatra

Envy over land

B. Roads

Connects international and local roads

C. Water

Three springs

III. QUMRAN

Dead Sea Scrolls

IV. VALLEY OF ACHOR

A. Hosea

Image of vineyards in the wilderness

B. Baptism of Jesus

Other biblical examples of water splitting and birds involved

REFLECTION QUESTIONS

1. Where is the Aravah located? What conditions make it possible for caravans to travel here? What mineral was mined here? What was it used for in biblical times?

2. Where is the Dead See located in relation to the Aravah? What imagery does Jeremiah use in Jeremiah 17:6? How is this descriptive of the land around the Dead Sea? In what ways is this the opposite of the imagery in Jeremiah 17:7? In what ways are these verses true of the way you are living your life?

3. What trees grow near the Dead Sea? What do they produce? How are they used as a metaphor in Scripture?

4. Where was bitumen found? What did it look like? What was it used for? Why was it a popular item in Egypt?

5. Why was balsam considered valuable? What did the people of Israel do to attempt to prevent the Romans from getting it?

6. Why was Masada an unlikely place to build a palace? Who built it? What features did it include that were obscenely luxurious?

7. Where is En Gedi? What is located there? In what way is this a contrast to the surrounding area? What is a spiritual application that you can make in reference to Dr. Parker's comment about the difference between looking at living water and being immersed in living water?

8. What is remarkable about the ability of ibeks to thrive in the terrain they live in? How does Habakkuk use this as a metaphor to teach a spiritual truth?

9. When you read Psalm 63, how does knowing that David is in the area of En Gedi help you better understand the meaning of the imagery he used?

10. Why did Herod hate Cleopatra? What happened when Octavian became the emperor of Rome?

11. Which roads connect near the city of Jericho? What are the destinations of the local roads?

12. What is strategic about Jericho besides the roads

13. Where is Qumran in relation to Jericho? Why is it a significant archaeological site?

14. What significant event happened in the Valley of Achor when the people of Israel were first entering the promised land (Joshua 7)? What is the contrast in the imagery that Hosea uses in Hosea 2?

15. What other events in the Bible have similar imagery to the baptism of Jesus? What do they have in common?

16. What biblical events happened earlier in the same place that Jesus was baptized? How does connecting these events bring added weight and significance to the place and the event of the baptism of Jesus?

8

Hill Country of Judah

I. **HILL COUNTRY OF JUDAH**

   A. **Rainfall**

      More on the western slope, less on the eastern slope

   B. **Soil**

      Cenomanian

C. Agriculture

Known for grapes

II. HEBRON

A. Roads

Significant local roads

B. Natural capital of the Judean hill country

Elevated on a plateau

C. Biblical events

Abraham, Jacob, Caleb, David, etc.

III. BETHLEHEM

Small town on the edge of the wilderness

IV. TEKOA

Hometown of Amos

REFLECTION QUESTIONS

1. What is the typical yearly rainfall on the western slopes of the Judean hills? What crops will this support? Why is there less rainfall on the eastern slopes?

2. What type of soil is common in this area? Why is it good for agriculture?

3. What crop is this area known for? In what ways is it used as a metaphor in Isaiah 5 and Psalm 80? What do people familiar with the Hebrew Scriptures understand Jesus to mean in John 15?

4. Why is Hebron considered the natural capital of the Judean hill country?

5. What are some biblical events that occurred near Hebron? Why is each of them significant?

6.   Where is Bethlehem located? Why was Bethlehem considered less significant than other cities in Israel? Why is it considered a place of great significance?

7.   Why and in what ways did people diversify their economic activities in Bethlehem? How does this fit with the biblical accounts of Naomi and her descendants?

8.   Who is the prophet from Tekoa? Why did people reject his message? How does he respond to them? What does his response tell you about the geography of Tekoa?

9

Historical Background of Jerusalem

I.   BENJAMIN

A. Jerusalem

1. Sorek Wadi System

West of Jerusalem

2. Mount of Olives

East of Jerusalem

3. **Valleys**

Kidron, Central and Hinnom

4. **Hill**

Eastern and western

B. **History of people of Israel living in Jerusalem**

Original inhabitants were Jebusites

II. **DAVID**

Moved the capital city from Hebron to Jerusalem

III.   STORIES ABOUT JERUSALEM

"Gey Ben Hinnom," Gehenna

REFLECTION QUESTIONS

1.   Where is Jerusalem located in relation to Engedi, Hebron and Jerusalem?

2.   What is the geological barrier to the west of Jerusalem? Describe why it is a barrier. What is the geological barrier to the east and what is beyond it?

3. What town was Jeremiah from? How does that explain the imagery that he uses?

4. What are the main valleys in Jerusalem and where are they located?

5. Where are the two major hills in Jerusalem located? How does Dr. Parker describe them? Why is the Eastern hill more popular to live on than the Western hill?

6. What is the difference in the terrain and the Philistine coastal plain? How is this reflected in the way people in these areas view and treat outsiders?

7. What geographical feature is the dividing line between Benjamin and Judah? What are some of the possible reasons that David chose Jerusalem as the capital city of the nation?

8. What are the parallels that Dr. Parker makes with David leaving and reentering Jerusalem and Ezekiel's prophecy in Ezekiel 9? What landmarks are mentioned that help you visualize what is happening in each situation?

9. How does understanding the geography around Jerusalem help you understand the meaning of the prophecy in Ezekiel 47? What imagery does this passage use to show the power of living water? In what ways are you currently experiencing God's living water in your life?

10. How did the Valley of Hinnom develop connotations that associated it with hell? Why is it used to show the contrast between times when the people of Israel were faithful to God and times when they were unfaithful? What is a current area of your life in which God wants you to return to being faithful to him?

10

Jerusalem in the First Century

I. HEROD THE GREAT

A. The temple

Large temple, one God, no statues

B. Herod's palace

Western hill, higher than the temple

II. CONTEXT OF FIRST-CENTURY JERUSALEM

A. Wealthy people

Wanted to be near power

B. Public miqveh near the temple

Ceremonial cleansing before entering the temple

C. Antonia Fortress

Roman fort adjacent to the temple and overlooking it

III. PASSION NARRATIVE

Jesus entering the city from the Mount of Olives

REFLECTION QUESTIONS

1. What happened to Solomon's temple in the 4th century BC? What did Ezra and Nehemiah do? What was the condition of the temple when Herod the Great became king? What nationality was Herod? Why did he build a new temple? How did he do it? Why was it different from other temples in the world at that time? How does worshipping God and living by faith set you apart from other religions and philosophies?

2. Where did Herod build his palace? Where was it in relation to the temple? What does this tell you about Herod?

3. Who were the wealthy people and where did they live? Why did they want to live there?

4. What was the purpose of the miqveh? Where were they located? Do you have a process for preparing yourself to come into the presence of God to worship him?

5. Where was the Antonia Fortress built? Why was this a strategic location? Why was it difficult for the people of Israel to see a military fortress when they came to worship at the temple? What symbols of political and economic power do you often see? What do you do to remind yourself of what God has done in the past and what he is doing in the present in your life and in the world?

6. What was the event that began the celebration of
    Hanukkah? Why would the coming of Jesus to Jerusalem
    just before his crucifixion remind people of this event?

7. What prophecies was Jesus fulfilling when he came up
    from Jericho, through the wilderness, over the Mount of
    Olives and into Jerusalem? Why was riding on a donkey
    also significant?

8. What insights did you get from understanding the
    geography involved in the trials of Jesus that happened
    the night before his crucifixion?

11

Benjamin

I. LOCATION

   A. Cities

   B. Jerusalem, Bethel, Jericho, Gezer

   C. Roads

   D. Intersection of east-west and north-south roads

E. People

F. Mighty warriors

G. Gibeon

H. Created a deception to save themselves

II.   CENTRAL BENJAMIN PLATEAU

Gibeon, Mizpah, Ramah and Gibeah

REFLECTION QUESTIONS

1.   What are the cities that define the boundaries of the land
     of the tribe of Benjamin?

2. What roads run through Benjamin? Why is the location of the roads strategic?

3. What are the descriptions of the people of Benjamin that indicate that many of them were, "mighty men?" What are possible reasons for this? What applications might this have for you spiritually when you think about how you get proficient at sharing and living out your faith?

4. Who were Asa and Baasha? Why were they fighting over Ramah? What was the result?

12

The Shephelah

I. GEOLOGICAL FEATURES

Between the hill country and the coastal plain

II. ROADS

Natural road created by the Senonian rock

III. VALLEYS

Aijalon, Sorek, Elah, Guvrin, Lachish, Adoriam

IV. INTERNATIONAL ROUTES

Influence of Egypt

V. CITY LISTS

Strategic locations

VI. PROPHETS

A. Micah

Passionate rhetoric

B. Isaiah

Spoke often to the elite

REFLECTION QUESTIONS

1. What is the meaning of the word "shephelah?" Why was it given this name?

2. What kind of rock is visible here? Why is it a good agricultural zone? Why is it an area that people often fought over to gain control?

3. What are the six valleys that Dr. Parker mentions?

4.   What were some of the battles in and around the Aijalon Valley? Why was this land worth fighting over?

5.   What city did Pharaoh conquer and give as a gift to Solomon? Why did he do this?

6.   What are some reasons to consider the Elah Valley as second in significance to the Aijalon Valley?

7. What was significant about the food items that Jesse sent with David to give to his brothers? In addition to the safety of his sons, why might Jesse have had an interest in the outcome of the battle with the Philistines?

8. What does, "Shaaraim" mean in Hebrew? Why is this an unusual name for a city? Why is this city mentioned in the story describing the aftermath of the battle with David and Goliath?

9. What is significant about the cities that Rehoboam fortifies against Egypt, listed in 2 Chronicles 11:5-11?

10. When comparing Micah and Isaiah, how do the differences in their messages and the way they communicate them reflect where they come from? When you read Micah and Isaiah, how does this help you to understand what they were saying and how you can apply it to your life? What is one passage from each of these books that is meaningful to you?

13

The Sharon Plain and Mount Carmel

I.   SHARON PLAIN

    A. **Not many cities**

       Swampy, so not easy to inhabit

    B. **Kurkar Ridges**

       Three ridges parallel to the coastline

II. THE PLAIN OF DOR

Between Sharon Plain and Mt. Carmel

III. MT. CARMEL

Considered to be the place where the earth meets the heavens

IV. CAESAREA

Built on the coast by Herod the Great

V. JORDAN RIVER VALLEY

Between the sea of Galilee and the Dead Sea

REFLECTION QUESTIONS

1. What are the two tribes that are known as the House of Joseph? Why do you think Jacob conferred a double blessing on his youngest son, Joseph, instead of his oldest son, Reuben? (cf. Genesis 48:1-7)?

2. Where is the Yarkon river located? Why does it affect the route of the coastal highway?

3. What type of rock is found in the western part of this region? How does that affect the lifestyle of the people that live here?

4. What geographical features define the Sharon Plain? Why were there few cities in this region during biblical times? Why are there cities there now? What crops is it known for?

5. Where is the Plain of Dor and how is it formed? Why doesn't the international road go through here?

6. What type of soil is visible on the western part of Mt. Carmel? Why was this significant to the Canaanites?

7. What is the soil and the geography like on the eastern side of Mt. Carmel?

8. What are the three passageways through Mt. Carmel that people often took? What are the destinations and routes of each one?

9. Why did Herod build the city of Caesarea? What construction method did he use to make the harbor? What was the water source for the city? How did this affect the trade routes?

10. What are the geographical features that define the Jordan River Valley?

11. What roads and passageways give people access to different places in the House of Joseph? How is this different from the tribal areas of Judah and Benjamin?

14

The Hill Country of Joseph

I. ROADS

Local roads

II. EARLY DAYS

A. Shiloh

Off the road with hills around it

B. Abraham's journey

Abraham settles in Shechem

C. Open countryside

Agriculture, commerce and travel

D. Mt. Gerizim and Mt. Ebal

Reminder of the covenant

E. Shechem stories

Abraham, Jacob, Joseph, Joshua

III. CHOSEN PLACE

Movement into the chosen place and out from the chosen place

IV. TIRZAH

Jeroboam moves the capital from Shechem

REFLECTION QUESTIONS

1. Why does the hill country of the House of Joseph have abundant resources compared to other areas in Israel? Why is that consistent with this area having numerous local roads?

2. Why is Shiloh important as a religious center when the people of Israel return to the promised land? Why does Joshua meet at Shiloh with the leaders of each tribe before they settle in the land? What role do the women of Shiloh have in preserving the tribe of Benjamin?

3. Since the geography of this area is more open than the hill country of the south, what are the advantages and liabilities that were faced by the people living here? How is this different from the people that lived in the hill country? What is a situation in your life where you are having a positive impact on others? What is a situation where you are allowing people to have a negative impact on you?

4. What are the two mountains that are near Shechem? What did the people of Israel do on the mountains when they first entered the land? What connection did this have to Mount Sinai? Why is the proximity of the mountains and their location significant? What are some specific habits that you have or items that you have that remind you of what God has done for you in the past? What is a current situation in your life in which these reminders help you to live by faith?

5. What is the purpose of the Chosen Place? How is it similar on a personal scale to the purpose of the Abrahamic Covenant on a national scale?

6. What are the "sins of Jeroboam?" How did he do it in a way that made it easier to follow the changes he made? What is something that we have changed in the church and/or society that is different from the way God intended it? What is something that you are doing in your life that you need to correct?

15

Samaria

I. **SAMARIA**

    A. **The city**

        Omri made it the capital city

    B. **Assyrian influence**

        Remove the people they conquer and bring in other people

C. Babylonian influence

Focus on recording and preserving their history and culture

D. Persian influence

Polytheistic and permissive

E. Rebuilding the temple in Jerusalem

Ezra, Nehemiah and Judeans

F. Religious heritage of the people in Samaria

The remnant who did not go into captivity

II. SHECHEM VS. JERUSALEM

A. Jesus walks through Samaria

Jesus chooses to go through Samaria to get to Galilee

B. Herod the Great's three sons

Three different regions that they governed

REFLECTION QUESTIONS

1. What were some advantages of Omri changing the capital city to Samaria? What did Herod the Great build there? Why?

2. When Assyria conquered an area, what was their strategy for subjugating it? How does this affect the way people worshipped God in this area?

3. Why was it difficult for the people of Israel to preserve their worship of God and religious practices during their captivity in Babylon? What did they do about it? What do you do to worship God authentically while living in a secular culture?

4. Why was there a conflict between the tribe of Judah and the northern tribes of Israel when Persia allows the Judeans to return and rebuild the temple in Jerusalem?

5. Who was the leader that began to rebuild the temple in Samaria? How did he persuade a priest from Judah to help him? What were the similarities and differences of the religious heritage of the Samaritans and the people of Judah?

6. What do the Jews cite as two references to Jerusalem in the Torah? Why do the Samaritans disagree? How does this affect the belief of each group about where the temple to God should be built?

7. Why was it unusual that Jesus would walk through Samaria? Why was the woman at the well in the middle of the day? What can we learn from the conversation that she has with Jesus?

16

Acco Plain

I. LOCATION

North of Mt. Carmel

II. UPPER AND LOWER GALILEE

Divided by the Bet HaKerem Ridge

III. LOWER GALILEE

A. Terrain and climate

Abundance of water and good soil

B. Roads

Local roads connecting to international roads

C. Valleys

Bet Netofa, Turan, Jezreel

D. Galilee of the gentiles

The first area affected by the Assyrian onslaught

REFLECTION QUESTIONS

1. What nations near Israel were known for using the sea for transporting goods for trade? In the writings of the people of Israel, how do they describe the sea?

2. What is alluvial soil? Why is alluvial soil abundant on the Acco Plain?

3. What is the difference in elevation of the two Galilees? What is the geographical feature that separates these two areas?

4. What is the weather and vegetation like in Upper Galilee? Why?

5. What type of geographical feature is the Horns of Hittim? How did it affect the area of Lower Galilee?

6. What factors in Lower Galilee make it a productive place for agriculture? Why is it a good place for roads? What makes it such a desirable place to live and travel compared to Judah and upper Galilee?

7. What are the three major valleys in Lower Galilee? What are the ridges that define them?

8. How did Assyria influence "gentile Galilee?" In what time period did this happen? What were the promises that Isaiah prophesied that were fulfilled during that time? How was the fulfillment in Isaiah's time similar to the way Christ fulfilled them in his ministry? What are you doing in your life and in your faith community to live in a way that continues to bring the light of God into the lives of people in the world around you?

9. Why was the influence of the Greek empire on the people of Israel different from the influence of the Egyptian, Assyrian, Babylonian and Persian Empires? What is one example in the New Testament of Greek influence on the culture of the people of Israel? In what areas are you currently challenged in how to live by faith in your culture? What is one thing that God has revealed to you recently that you have put into practice?

17

Jezreel and Herod Valleys

I. THE MOUNTAINS

Mt. Carmel, Mt. Gilboa, Mt. Tabor, Nazareth Ridge

II. CONNECTING POINTS

The valleys create connecting points

III. STORIES THAT HAPPENED NEAR THE JEZREEL VALLEY

A. 1 Kings 18

Elijah and the priests of Baal and Mt. Carmel

B. Megiddo

Josiah tries to stop the Egyptians

C. Jezreel

Ahab steals the vineyard of Naboth

D. Herod Valley

Springs of Herod where Gideon decreased the number of troops

E. Mt. Gilboa

The Philistines kill Saul and his son, Jonathan

F. Mt. Tabor

Deborah the judge

G. Nazareth

Small city but near international activity

H. Elisha and Jesus

Similar stories in the same places

I. Ahab

Ahab married Jezebel, who was the daughter of the king of Sidon

J. Beth-shan

Egyptian influence

K. Jabesh-Gilead and Saul

The people from Jabesh-Gilead felt connected to Saul

L. Roman Influence

Buildings and culture

IV. DESCRIPTION OF A TEL

Archaeological dig

REFLECTION QUESTIONS

1. What are the mountains that form the Jezreel and Herod Valleys? Why does Dr. Parker describe the Jezreel Valley as a "revolving door?" Why would this area be a strategic place to control?

2. When the Egyptians under Tutmos III wanted to control the Jezreel and Herod Valleys, what people group were they taking it from? As they were coming from the south, what choices did they have for routes that would get them to the Jezreel Valley? Which route did they choose? Why was it the riskiest? What was the result? What reason did Tutmos III give for making this choice? When has God called you to make a risky decision and you saw a positive result? In what way is God calling you to live by faith now by making a decision that seems risky?

3. Until recently, why were there parts of the Jezreel Valley that were difficult to travel in and to farm? Why is it different now?

4. In I Kings 18, why is it significant that God tells Elijah to have the confrontation with the prophets of Baal on Mt. Carmel? What is the significance of Elijah challenging the prophets of Baal to have their god send lightning to burn their sacrifice? Why did Elijah tell Ahab to travel to his palace in Jezreel before the rain came? How was Elijah able to get there before Ahab?

5. In Judges 4 and 5, who is in charge of the army of the people of Israel? Who are they fighting against? How does God turn their disadvantage into an advantage? What happened to Sisera?

6. What are the similarities between the miracles that Elisha did with the son of the Shunamite woman and with Naaman, and the miracles that Jesus did with the son of the woman at Nain and the 10 lepers? How is the geography significant? Why would first-century people of Israel see them as a confirmation that Jesus is the Messiah?

7. When Ahab married Jezebel, what political and economic implications did this have?

8. What are some possible reasons why the people of Jabesh-Gilead would take the risk of going to the city of an enemy to recover the dead bodies of Saul and his sons so they could bury them honorably?

18

Sea of Galilee

I. "SEA" OF GALILEE

Freshwater body of water

II. GENNESARET

On the western shore of the Sea of Galilee

III. ROSH PINA SIL

Basalt to the north of the Sea of Galilee

IV. HEBREW BIBLE STORIES

Gesher and Hazor

V. NEW TESTAMENT STORIES

Ministry of Jesus

VI. CAPERNAUM

A. Shoreline of the Sea of Galilee

Northwest shore

B. Mathew 4:15-17 and Isaiah 9:1-2

The ministry of Jesus in in Zebulun and Naphtali

C. Followers of Jesus

Different occupations and perspectives

D. Response to miracles

Depends whether Jesus was in Israel or Decapolis

E. Jesus uses local geography to teach

The tower in Tiberias

REFLECTION QUESTIONS

1. Why is the Sea of Galilee named a "sea" since it is fresh water?

2. In what ways did Josephus describe the area around Gennesaret and the Sea of Galilee as an ideal place?

3. In what ways is the geography around the Sea of Galilee different from Jerusalem? How might this make a difference in the mindset of the people living in these places? What are some examples in the Gospels showing how this plays out?

4. What is the Rosh Pina Sil? Where is it located? How was it formed? How does it affect the Jordan River and the Sea of Galilee?

5. Why does David marry a woman from Gesher? Who is her son? Why does it make sense that her son runs "north" when he is in conflict with David?

6. Why does the location of the roads change from the time of the Hebrew Bible to New Testament times? What are some noticeable changes around the Sea of Galilee?

7. Who built Tiberias? Where does this city get its name?

8.   What are the clues from archaeology that Capernaum was a diverse community?

9.   When you compare the geography of Nazareth and Capernaum, what are the differences that would cause people in these cities to have different attitudes, mindsets and theologies? What are some examples from the ministry of Jesus that indicate that he was spending more time in the area of Capernaum than Nazareth?

10. In John 7:1, should it be translated that the, "Jews" were seeking to kill Jesus or that the, "Judeans" were trying to kill Jesus? Why? Why does it make a difference?

11. What were the three different worldview populations that Jesus had easy access to from Capernaum? As Jesus takes his disciples to these places, how does it prepare them for taking the gospel throughout the world after he is gone? What different people groups are you purposefully engaging with in your sphere of influence? Who are you choosing to partner with to disciple in this process?

12. In Matthew 4:16 when Jesus goes from Nazareth to Capernaum, why does Matthew see a connection to Isaiah 9:1,2? What are you doing to help people in your sphere of influence to make this connection today?

13. What was there about the different backgrounds of the disciples that would have made it challenging to get along and develop relationships? Why do you think Jesus chose people from such diverse backgrounds? How is that a model for you today in how you interact with and value others in your church, your community and the world?

14. In what geographical areas does Jesus tell people to not spread the word that he is the Messiah? In what areas does Jesus tell people to tell everyone? Why the difference?

15. How does Jesus use local geography to illustrate and emphasize different points that he is making in the Sermon on the Mount? How does seeing these connections make the Sermon on the Mount more meaningful to you?

16. What two parables did Jesus tell that were likely referring to bad decisions that Herod Antipas had made? What scriptural principal could you teach in a similar way by referring to an example in current events?

19

Huleh Basin

I.   WATER SOURCES

Rainwater, runoff and springs

II.   HAZOR

Northern oriented for trade

III.   ABEL-BET MAACAH

Wise woman of Abel-bet Maacah

IV. DAN

A. Tribal allotment

Changed locations

B. Abraham

Abraham defended his family

C. Jeroboam

Made Dan a place of worship

D. Gateway in the north

The first city that comes in contact with an invading force

V. CAESAREA PHILLIPPI

Herod Phillip built a temple dedicated to Caesar

VI. REVIEW

REFLECTION QUESTIONS

1. What are the sources of water in the Huleh Basin? How is
    the soil formed there? What is the challenge for growing
    crops here and managing the ecosystem here?

2. What biblical stories involve the city of Hazor? How
    do these stories indicate the economic and strategic
    importance of Hazor?

3. What is there about the location of Abel-bet Maacah that makes it strategic?

4. What can we learn from the story in 2 Samuel 20:15ff about Abel-bet Maacah in particular and the culture of the people of Israel in general?

5. When the people of Israel first came to the promised land, where was the allotment for the tribe of Dan? Why didn't it work out well? What did the people of the tribe of Dan do about it?

6. What is unique about the design of the gate at Dan that was built about the time of Abraham? What does it tell you about the writers of the Hebrew Bible that the city is referred to as Dan in Genesis 14:14-15?

7. In Matthew 16 when Jesus asks the disciples who people say that he is, why is it significant that they are in Caesarea Phillippi? When Jesus says about his church that, "the gates of Hades will not overcome it," who is on the offense? Why does this make a difference? How does this make a difference as you interact with people in your sphere of influence and participate in your community of faith?

8. What rabbinical practice is Jesus referring to by "binding and loosing?" Why was this a critical teaching for the disciples when they later were forming the church?

9. What is the contrast that Jesus is making in Matthew 16 between the human power and authority symbolized in the buildings in Caesarea Phillippi and the suffering servant Messiah that he came to be and is modeling as a lifestyle for the disciples?

20

Going Out From the Land

I. JOURNEY

   A. **Jesus to Jerusalem in Luke 9-19**

      Review of the ministry of Jesus ending at Jerusalem

   B. **The Gospel going out from Jerusalem Acts 1:8**

      The Gospel affecting different geographical areas in concentric circles

II. RESTORATION

A. Coming of the Holy Spirit

The Holy Spirit comes in a way that God has appeared in the past

B. Proclamation of the gospel

The gospel preached in a way that everyone could understand

C. Expanding to include others

People groups represented from all the continents

REFLECTION QUESTIONS

1. What journey does Luke trace in chapters 9-19 of his Gospel? What are some of the stops along the way? What is the journey he traces in the book of Acts? What are some of the stops along the way?

2. What Jewish holiday was the disciples preparing to celebrate that took place 7 weeks after the death of Jesus? How did people of Israel at this time connect his holiday with Mt. Sinai? How was theophany at Mt. Sinai similar to what happened with the coming of the Holy Spirit at Pentecost?

3. When Peter gives his sermon in Acts chapter 2, what is his main emphasis? What does he say that is an indication that he is speaking primarily to a Jewish audience? When 3,000 people respond to the message of the gospel that day and are saved, how is that connected to the events on Mt. Sinai?

4. What is the tension in the message of the disciples of "going out" to bring the gospel to all people and all cultures and also to "remember" that what Jesus did is anchored in Jerusalem?

21

Epilogue

I.   JOHN CHAPTER 6

Note the location and the details in the story

II.   MARK 8

Note the location and the details in the story

REFLECTION QUESTIONS

1. In the story of the feeding of the thousands in John 6, what details in the story does John give that tells you what time of year it is? How does this scenario connect in the minds of the people there to the first Passover and their journey out of Egypt? How is John using this story to show that Jesus is the Messiah?

2. In the story of the feeding of the thousands in Mark 8, why are the details different? How is the number 7 used and why is it significant to readers of the Hebrew Bible?

Made in the USA
Middletown, DE
31 August 2023

37712132R00080